THE ULTIMATE
Hummingbird
BOOK FOR KIDS

Copyright © 2023 by Jenny Kellett

www.bellanovabooks.com

All rights reserved. No part of this book may be reproduced in any form by any electronic or mechanical means including photocopying, recording, or information storage and retrieval without permission in writing from the author.

Imprint: Bellanova Books

CONTENTS

Introduction 4
Types of Hummingbirds 8
Anatomy of a Hummingbird 19
Feeding Habits 26
Migration Patterns 34
Breeding & Reproduction 41
Hummingbird Threats 48
What can we do to help? 52
Hummingbirds in Culture 56
Watching and Attracting Hummingbirds 60
Hummingbird Fun Facts 68
Hummingbird Quiz 88
Answers 92
Word search 94
Solution 96
Sources 97

INTRODUCTION

Welcome to the exciting world of hummingbirds, some of the most fascinating and unique creatures on our planet. In this first chapter, we'll take a quick look at what makes hummingbirds so special, their physical features, and where you might find them.

Are you ready to dive into the colorful and fast-paced world of these tiny birds? **Let's go!**

WHAT IS A HUMMINGBIRD?

First things first, what exactly is a hummingbird? Hummingbirds are small birds belonging to the family **Trochilidae**. They are known for their remarkable flying abilities and their love for sweet nectar. You might have even seen one zooming around your garden on a sunny day!

SIZE AND COLORS

One of the most amazing things about hummingbirds is their size. They are incredibly small, with the **Bee hummingbird** being the smallest species, measuring only about 2 inches (5 cm) long. Even the largest species, the **Giant hummingbird**, is only about 8 inches (20 cm) long. Don't let their size fool you, though; these little birds are full of energy and surprises.

Hummingbirds come in a dazzling array of colors, from the iridescent blues and greens of the **Violet-crowned Woodnymph** to the shimmering reds and oranges of the **Ruby-throated Hummingbird**. Their feathers catch the light in a way that makes them appear to change color as they move - a breathtaking sight to see!

WHERE TO FIND HUMMINGBIRDS

These incredible birds can be found in a variety of environments across the Americas, from the tropical rainforests of South America to the mountains of North America. In fact, there are over 300 different species of hummingbirds, each with their own unique characteristics and habitats. No matter where you are in the Americas, you have a good chance of spotting one of these delightful creatures!

DISCOVERING THE WORLD OF HUMMINGBIRDS

Now that you know a little bit about what hummingbirds are, you're probably eager to learn more about their unique features, types, and habits. Don't worry - we've got you covered! In the following chapters, we'll explore various aspects of hummingbirds, such as their anatomy, feeding habits, migration patterns, and much more.

TYPES OF HUMMINGBIRDS

Now that we know a bit about hummingbirds, let's dive into the different types of hummingbirds that live on our planet. With over 300 species, each with their own unique colors, sizes, and habitats, there's a lot to learn!

While all hummingbirds belong to the same family, **Trochilidae**, they are further divided into about 110 genera. Each genus contains species that share similar characteristics or adaptations, making it easier for scientists to study and understand their relationships. Let's take a look at some of the most common species of hummingbirds.

RUBY-THROATED HUMMINGBIRD

One of the most well-known species of hummingbirds is the Ruby-throated hummingbird (**Archilochus colubris**). It is the only species that breeds in eastern North America, making it a familiar sight in gardens and backyards during the warmer months. Males have a bright, iridescent red throat, which is where they get their name. These tiny birds, measuring just 3 to 3.5 inches (7.5-9 cm) long, love to feed on the nectar of red and orange flowers.

ANNA'S HUMMINGBIRD

Anna's hummingbird (**Calypte anna**) is a year-round resident along the western coast of North America, from Alaska to Baja California. They are medium-sized hummingbirds, with males displaying a stunning iridescent rose-pink throat and head.

Anna's hummingbirds are known for their incredible aerial displays during courtship, with males soaring high into the sky before diving down at impressive speeds to impress potential mates.

Did you know...?

Anna's hummingbirds are able to tolerate colder temperatures and have even been spotted in snowy conditions, which is quite unusual for hummingbirds.

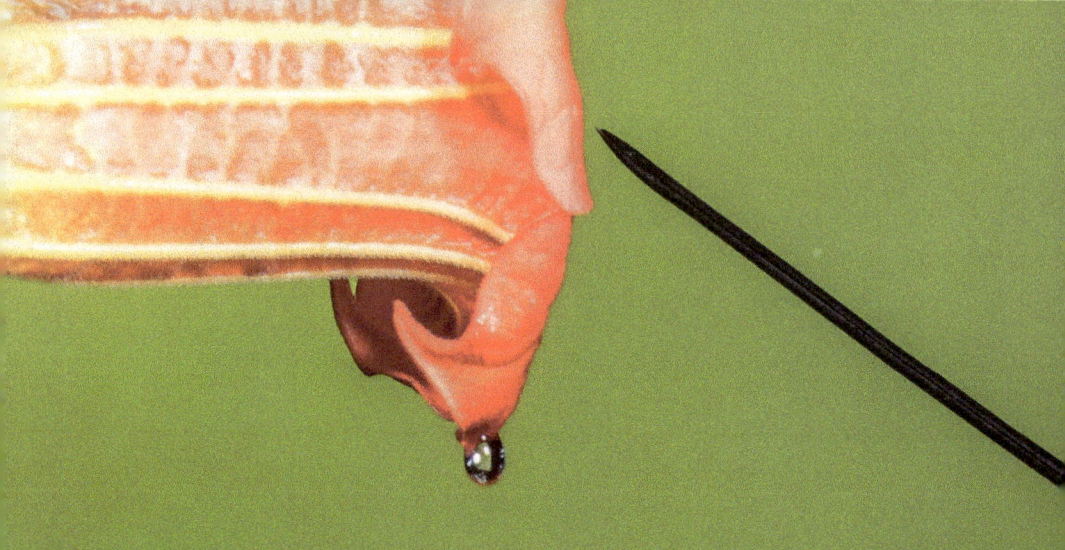

SWORD-BILLED HUMMINGBIRD

The Sword-billed hummingbird (**Ensifera ensifera**) is a truly unique species, found in the high Andean forests of South America. What sets this hummingbird apart is its long, straight bill, which can be longer than its body! This extraordinary adaptation allows the Sword-billed hummingbird to feed on long-tubed flowers that other hummingbirds cannot reach. Both males and females have striking green plumage with a hint of bronze.

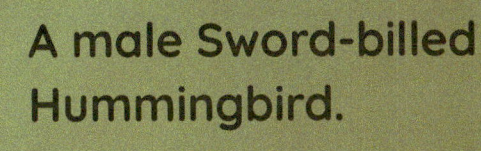

A male Sword-billed Hummingbird.

Image: Andy Morffew

BLACK-CHINNED HUMMINGBIRD

The Black-chinned hummingbird (**Archilochus alexandri**) is a small, adaptable bird found in the western United States, Mexico, and Central America. As their name suggests, the males have a black chin with a thin band of iridescent purple just below it. Black-chinned hummingbirds are often found in desert areas, feeding on a variety of nectar-rich flowers, as well as insects and spiders.

LONG-TAILED SYLPH

The Long-tailed Sylph (**Aglaiocercus kingii**) is a breathtaking species found in the cloud forests of Colombia. Males have iridescent green bodies with incredibly long, shimmering blue tail feathers that can be more than twice their body length! These stunning tail feathers are used in courtship displays to attract females. The Long-tailed Sylph primarily feeds on nectar but will also eat small insects.

WHITE-BOOTED RACKET-TAIL

The White-booted Racket-tail (Ocreatus underwoodii) is a small, captivating hummingbird found in the Andean cloud forests of Colombia, Ecuador, and northern Peru.

Both males and females have fluffy white leg "boots" that give them their name. Males also have unique racket-shaped tail feathers, with two elongated outer feathers that end in a round, flat disk. These birds are known for their agility in flight, often hovering and darting between flowers as they feed.

Image: Lip Kee

THE ULTIMATE HUMMINGBIRD

ANATOMY OF A HUMMINGBIRD

In this chapter, we're going to take a closer look at the fascinating anatomy of hummingbirds. These tiny birds have some truly remarkable physical adaptations that allow them to thrive in their environments.

From their wings and feathers to their beaks and tongues, let's discover what makes hummingbirds such extraordinary creatures.

WINGS: BUILT FOR SPEED & PRECISION

One of the most distinctive features of hummingbirds is their incredible flying abilities. They can hover, fly forwards, backwards, and even upside-down! All of this is made possible by their unique wing structure. Unlike most birds, hummingbirds have a ball-and-socket joint at their shoulders, which allows their wings to rotate in a full circle. This enables them to generate lift and thrust in any direction.

Additionally, their wings are shorter and stiffer than those of other birds, allowing them to flap at incredibly high speeds—up to 80 times per second in some species! This rapid wing movement creates the signature humming sound we associate with these birds and allows them to hover in place while feeding on nectar.

FEATHERS: A RAINBOW OF IRIDESCENT COLORS

The beautiful, iridescent colors of hummingbirds are one of their most striking features. These dazzling colors are created by microscopic plate-like structures within their feathers called "melanin platelets." These platelets are arranged in layers and reflect light in such a way that the colors appear to change depending on the angle of the light. This creates the shimmering, metallic effect we often see in hummingbird feathers.

TONGUES: DESIGNED FOR EFFICIENCY

Image: Henley Quadling

To extract nectar from flowers, hummingbirds have a highly specialized tongue. Their tongue is long and forked at the tip, with each side forming a tube-like structure. When a hummingbird inserts its tongue into a flower, the two sides of the tongue come together to create a channel that draws the nectar up and into the bird's mouth. This remarkable adaptation allows hummingbirds to feed quickly and efficiently, which is essential given their high energy demands.

HIGH METABOLISM: FUELING THEIR INCREDIBLE LIFESTYLES

Hummingbirds have the highest metabolism of any bird species, which means they need to consume a lot of energy to maintain their rapid wingbeats and constant activity. To meet these energy demands, they consume large quantities of nectar and insects, sometimes eating their body weight in food each day! To cope with their high metabolism, hummingbirds have a large heart relative to their body size, which pumps blood at an astonishing rate to deliver oxygen and nutrients throughout their bodies.

THE ULTIMATE HUMMINGBIRD BOOK

What, where and how hummingbirds eat

In this chapter, we will delve into the sweet world of hummingbird feeding habits, exploring the types of nectar and insects they consume, as well as the unique ways they use their beaks and tongues to extract nectar. Understanding these habits provides valuable insights into the daily lives of these dazzling creatures and the crucial role they play in their ecosystems.

Did you know…?

Hummingbirds can remember the locations of individual flowers and the timing of when they last fed from them! This allows them to follow a precise feeding route, known as "trap-lining," where they visit flowers in a specific sequence to maximize their nectar intake.

NECTAR: THE PRIMARY ENERGY SOURCE

Hummingbirds primarily feed on **nectar**, a sweet liquid produced by many flowering plants. Nectar is rich in sugar, providing the energy these birds need to fuel their high metabolism and support their rapid wingbeats. To get to the nectar, hummingbirds use their long beaks and specialized tongues, which we looked at in the previous chapter. They can consume up to their body weight in nectar each day, visiting hundreds or even thousands of flowers in search of this vital energy source!

INSECTS AND SPIDERS: A PROTEIN BOOST

While nectar provides the energy that hummingbirds need, it doesn't contain all the essential nutrients they need for growth and reproduction.

To supplement their diet, hummingbirds also feed on insects and spiders, which are an important source of protein, vitamins, and minerals. These small creatures make up about 10% of a hummingbird's diet, and they are usually caught in mid-air or plucked from leaves, branches, and spider webs. Common prey include flies, ants, aphids, and small beetles.

Did you know...?

Some flowers have evolved specifically to attract hummingbirds for pollination! These flowers are typically brightly colored (especially red), tubular-shaped, and have little to no scent, as hummingbirds rely on their keen eyesight, rather than their sense of smell, to locate flowers with nectar.

POLLINATION: A MUTUAL BENEFIT

As hummingbirds go about their day sipping nectar from flowers, they play a vital role in the pollination process. **Pollination** involves moving pollen from one part of a flower to another, which allows plants to create seeds and reproduce. When a hummingbird reaches into a flower for some nectar, its head brushes against the flower's pollen-bearing parts. As it visits more flowers, it transfers pollen between them, helping with pollination. This partnership between hummingbirds and flowers contributes to a diverse and healthy environment for all.

A white-throated hummingbird.

ADAPTATIONS FOR DIFFERENT FLOWERS

There are so many different species of hummingbirds, and each one has its own special way of getting to its favorite food - flower nectar! Some hummingbirds have long, curved beaks that let them reach deep into tube-shaped flowers, while others have shorter, straight beaks that make it easy to get nectar from open flowers. The cool part is that a hummingbird's beak is often just the right shape for the flowers in its neighborhood, showing how closely connected these birds are with their favorite snacks.

MIGRATION PATTERNS

Have you ever wondered how such tiny birds like hummingbirds can travel incredibly long distances? Well, get ready to be amazed! In this chapter, we'll explore the fascinating world of hummingbird migration. We'll learn about why they migrate, the routes they take, and the challenges they face during their journeys.

So, buckle up for a fast-paced adventure into the lives of these remarkable little travelers!

Why Do Hummingbirds Migrate?

The main reason hummingbirds migrate is to find food. As you know, they love nectar from flowers and munching on insects. But these yummy treats can be hard to find all year round in one place. So, to make sure they always have enough to eat, most hummingbirds travel to areas where flowers are blooming and insects are abundant.

Another reason for migration is the weather. Many hummingbirds don't like cold temperatures and can't survive in freezing conditions. By moving to warmer places, they can escape the chilly weather and find a cozy spot to spend the winter.

The Incredible Journey

Now, you might be thinking, "But how far do these tiny birds travel?" That's a great question! The answer depends on the species of hummingbird. Some might only travel a few hundred miles, while others, like the Ruby-throated Hummingbird (pictured right), can fly thousands of miles between their breeding grounds in North America and their winter homes in Central America. That's quite the trip!

One of the most jaw-dropping parts of the Ruby-throated Hummingbird's migration is their non-stop flight across the Gulf of Mexico. They have to fly about 500 miles (800 km) without stopping to rest or eat, and it can take up to 18 hours. Imagine doing that without a single snack break!

Challenges on the Way

Migrating is a tough job for hummingbirds, and they face many challenges along the way. One of the biggest hurdles is finding enough food to keep their energy levels up. They need to find flowers and insects as they travel, which can be tricky if their usual feeding spots are destroyed or changed by things like cities being built or climate change.

Another challenge is the weather itself. Strong winds, heavy rain, and extreme temperatures can make flying really tough for these little birds. Plus, they have to watch out for predators like birds of prey that might try to catch them during their journey.

But don't worry! Hummingbirds are amazing at adapting to these challenges. They have a built-in GPS (well, sort of) that helps them find their way. Scientists think they use the Earth's magnetic field, the position of the sun, and visual landmarks to navigate across long distances.

BREEDING & REPRODUCTION

It's time for another adventure in the fantastic world of hummingbirds! In this chapter, we'll take a closer look at the love lives of these tiny birds, from their amazing mating habits to their impressive nest-building skills, and even how they care for their adorable little babies. So, let's dive right in and discover the secrets of hummingbird romance and family life!

Mating: The Dance of Love

When it's time for hummingbirds to find a mate, they really know how to put on a show! Male hummingbirds perform incredible aerial displays to impress the females and win their hearts. They might zoom up high into the sky and then dive down at lightning-fast speeds, or they might show off their flying skills with daring loops and twists. The whole performance is like a dance in the air, designed to prove that they're the best match for the lucky lady.

Once a female hummingbird is impressed by a male's aerial dance, she'll choose him as her mate. But don't expect them to settle down together for life!

Hummingbirds don't form long-lasting pairs. Instead, after mating, the male goes off to look for other females, while the female gets ready to start her family.

BUILDING THE PERFECT NEST

When it comes to building a cozy home for her babies, a female hummingbird is a true artist. She carefully selects a safe and sheltered spot, usually on the branch of a tree or a bush. Then, she starts constructing the nest using a mix of plant materials, like leaves, moss, and tiny twigs. She holds everything together with sticky spider silk, which also helps the nest stretch as her babies grow.

The nest itself is a tiny masterpiece, only about the size of a walnut shell. It's soft and cushiony on the inside, often lined with soft materials like plant down or even feathers. This ensures that her babies will be warm and comfortable when they arrive.

Caring for the Little Ones

Once the nest is ready, the female lays one or two tiny eggs, each about the size of a pea. Then, she patiently keeps them warm by sitting on them for around 2 to 3 weeks until they hatch. During this time, she also makes sure to defend her nest from any threats, like other birds or curious humans who might get too close.

When the baby hummingbirds, called **chicks**, finally hatch, they're tiny, blind, and completely helpless. But their devoted mom is always there to take care of them! She feeds them a special mix of nectar and insects, which provides all the nutrients they need to grow strong and healthy. She also keeps them warm and clean until they're ready to venture out of the nest.

After about 3 to 4 weeks, the chicks are ready to leave the nest and start exploring the world. They learn to fly and find food on their own, and before long, they'll be all grown up and ready to find mates of their own. And so, the cycle of hummingbird life continues!

HUMMINGBIRD THREATS

As we've explored the amazing world of hummingbirds, it's clear that these tiny birds are truly remarkable creatures. But sadly, they face some big challenges in their lives. In this chapter, we'll learn about the threats that hummingbirds face, including habitat loss and climate change, and how we can help protect these beautiful birds and their homes.

Did you know...?

Hummingbirds' incredible speed and agility help them evade predators, but it also makes them highly susceptible to collisions with human-made structures like windows and wind turbines.

HABITAT LOSS: WHERE DID THE FLOWERS GO?

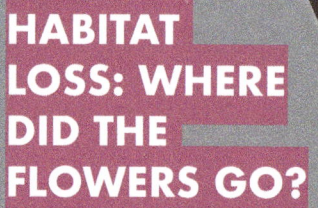

One of the biggest threats to hummingbirds is the loss of their natural habitats. As forests, meadows, and other natural areas are cleared for things like cities, roads, and farms, the flowers and plants that hummingbirds rely on for food and shelter disappear. Without these resources, hummingbirds struggle to find enough food, safe nesting spots, and suitable places to live.

CLIMATE CHANGE: A WORLD OUT OF BALANCE

Another major threat to hummingbirds is climate change. As the Earth's temperature rises, weather patterns change, causing some areas to become too hot, too cold, or too dry for

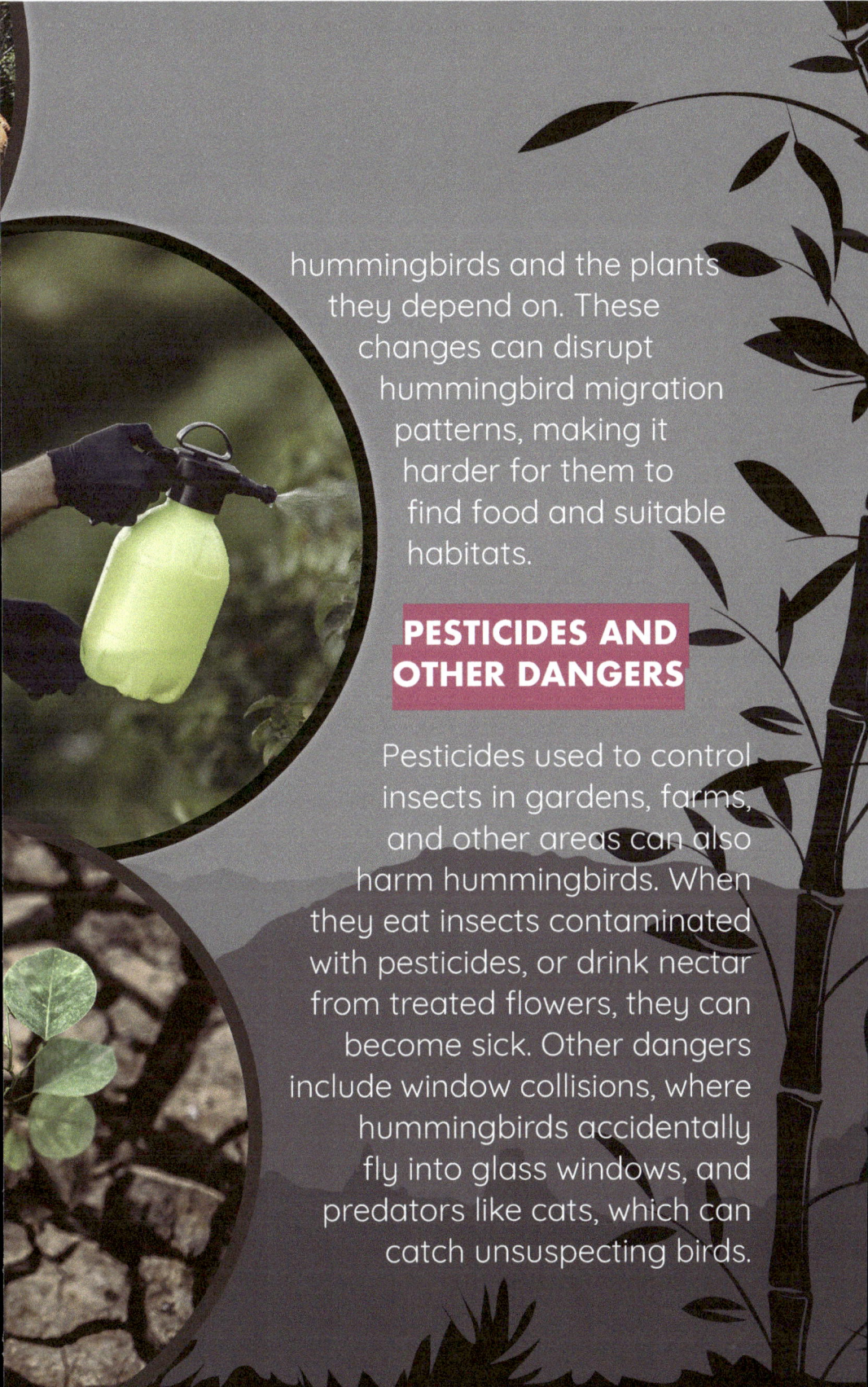

hummingbirds and the plants they depend on. These changes can disrupt hummingbird migration patterns, making it harder for them to find food and suitable habitats.

PESTICIDES AND OTHER DANGERS

Pesticides used to control insects in gardens, farms, and other areas can also harm hummingbirds. When they eat insects contaminated with pesticides, or drink nectar from treated flowers, they can become sick. Other dangers include window collisions, where hummingbirds accidentally fly into glass windows, and predators like cats, which can catch unsuspecting birds.

WHAT CAN <u>WE</u> DO TO HELP?

Everyone can play a role in ensuring a brighter future for hummingbirds.

Here are some ways you can contribute to their conservation and become a true Hummingbird Hero!

PLANT A HUMMINGBIRD-FRIENDLY GARDEN

By planting flowers that produce nectar, you can provide a valuable food source for hummingbirds. Choose native plants that are well-suited to your area and try to include a variety of flowers that bloom at different times of the year.

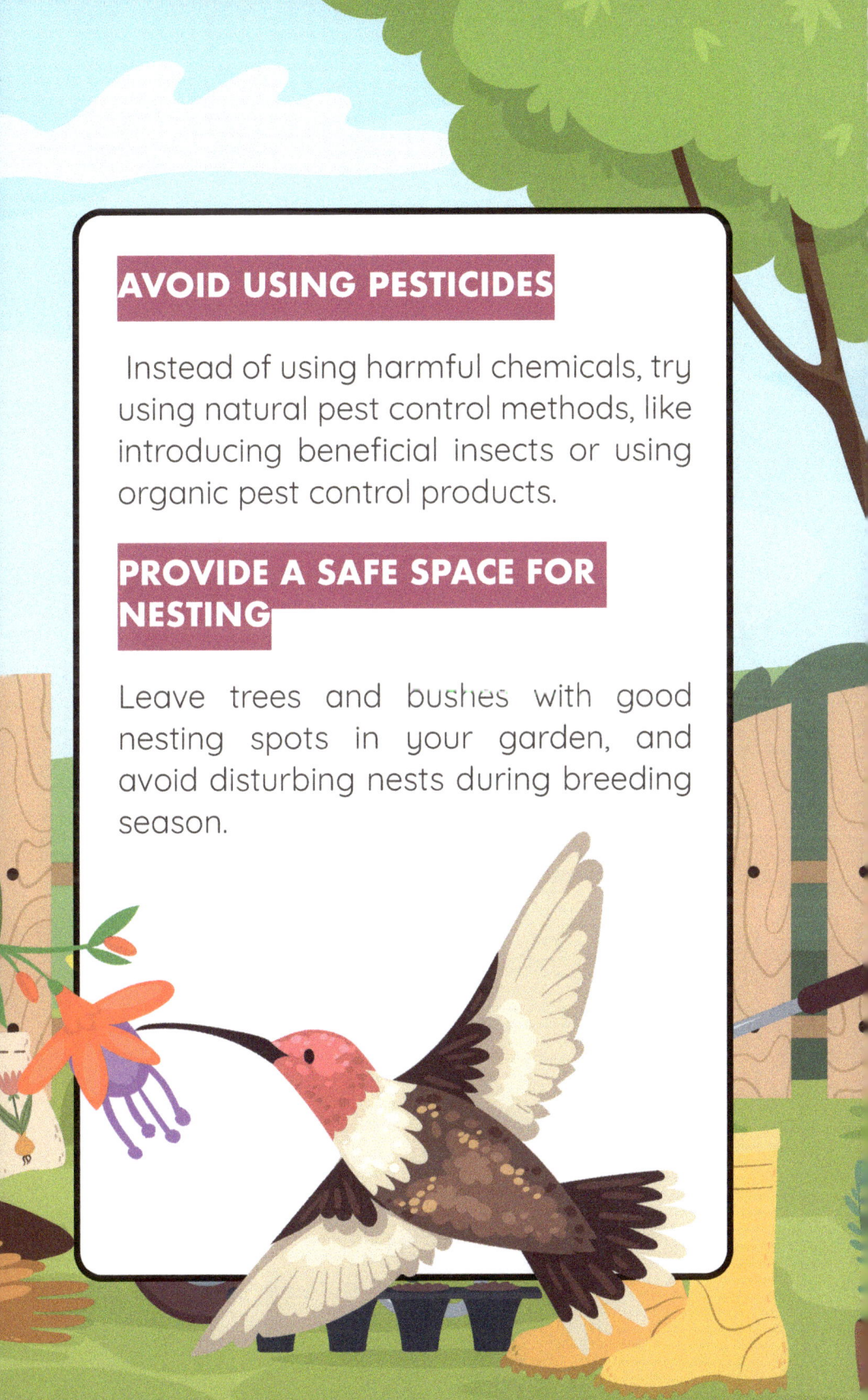

AVOID USING PESTICIDES

Instead of using harmful chemicals, try using natural pest control methods, like introducing beneficial insects or using organic pest control products.

PROVIDE A SAFE SPACE FOR NESTING

Leave trees and bushes with good nesting spots in your garden, and avoid disturbing nests during breeding season.

PROTECT YOUR WINDOWS

To prevent window collisions, you can add decals or other visual cues to your windows to help hummingbirds see them.

BE A HUMMINGBIRD ADVOCATE

Spread the word about the importance of protecting hummingbirds and their habitats by talking to your friends, family, and community members.

Every little bit helps! By getting involved in conservation efforts, spreading awareness, and making eco-friendly choices, you'll play a vital role in ensuring the survival of hummingbirds.

Together, we can make a difference and create a brighter future for hummingbirds and all the other amazing creatures that share our planet.

HUMMINGBIRDS IN CULTURE

Throughout history, hummingbirds have captured the hearts and imaginations of people all over the world. Their dazzling colors, incredible flying skills, and tiny size have made them symbols of beauty, love, and resilience in many cultures.

In this chapter, we'll take a journey through time and explore some of the myths, legends, and artistic expressions featuring our beloved hummingbirds.

ANCIENT LEGENDS AND MYTHS

Many indigenous peoples in the Americas have long admired hummingbirds and woven them into their stories and traditions. For example, the Aztec deity Huitzilopochtli (right) is symbolized as a hummingbird.

The Caribbean Taino viewed hummingbirds as symbols of love, happiness, and life, often celebrating them in art.

Various Native American tribes also have unique stories, such as the Pueblo people believing hummingbirds help bring rain, and the Cherokee seeing them as a symbol of joy and love.

HUMMINGBIRDS IN MODERN CULTURE

In modern culture, hummingbirds continue to captivate people with their beauty and grace. Their unique qualities and vibrant colors make them popular symbols for various organizations, businesses, and artistic expressions.

Caribbean Airlines: Caribbean Airlines has chosen the hummingbird as its logo, representing the spirit of the Caribbean, its people's warmth, and the natural beauty of the region.

"The Hummingbird Project" (2018):

This film revolves around two cousins who dream of building a fiber-optic cable between Kansas and New Jersey to gain a competitive edge in high-frequency trading. The hummingbird is used as a metaphor for speed and agility in this story about ambition and perseverance.

Hummingbird cake: This popular dessert, originating from the southern United States, is a moist, fruity cake made with bananas, pineapple, and pecans. The cake's name is thought to come from its sweetness, attracting people the same way hummingbirds are drawn to sweet nectar.

Image: NYT

WATCHING AND ATTRACTING HUMMINGBIRDS

After learning so much about the fascinating world of hummingbirds, you might be eager to see these incredible creatures in action for yourself. Whether you're observing them in the wild or inviting them into your own backyard, watching hummingbirds can be a magical experience.

In this chapter, we'll share some tips and tricks for observing these tiny wonders, as well as how to create a hummingbird-friendly haven in your own garden or balcony.

Watching Hummingbirds in the Wild

If you're lucky enough to live in an area where hummingbirds can be found, there are a few simple things you can do to increase your chances of spotting these beautiful birds:

Timing is everything:

Hummingbirds are most active during the early morning and late afternoon, so plan your birdwatching adventures during these times for the best chance of seeing them.

Be patient and stay still:

Like all birds, hummingbirds can be scared of humans. Find a quiet spot near some flowers or a feeder, and sit or stand as still as possible. With a little patience, you might be rewarded with a close-up view of a hummingbird in action.

Listen for their sounds:

Hummingbirds aren't just beautiful to look at; they also make unique sounds. Keep your ears open for their high-pitched chirps and the buzzing sound of their wings as they zip around.

Attracting Hummingbirds to Your Garden

If you'd like to see hummingbirds in your own backyard, here are a few things you can do to make your garden more appealing to these tiny guests:

Plant a hummingbird buffet:

Choose a variety of flowering plants that produce nectar, which is the main source of food for hummingbirds. Some great options include trumpet vine, bee balm, salvia, and fuchsia. Aim for a mix of plants that bloom at different times, so there's always something tasty on the menu.

Set up a feeder:

You can also provide an extra source of food by setting up a hummingbird feeder filled with sugar water. Be sure to clean the feeder regularly to prevent the growth of harmful bacteria, and replace the sugar water every few days.

Offer a place to perch:

Hummingbirds need to rest their wings from time to time. Provide them with small branches or other perches where they can take a break between meals.

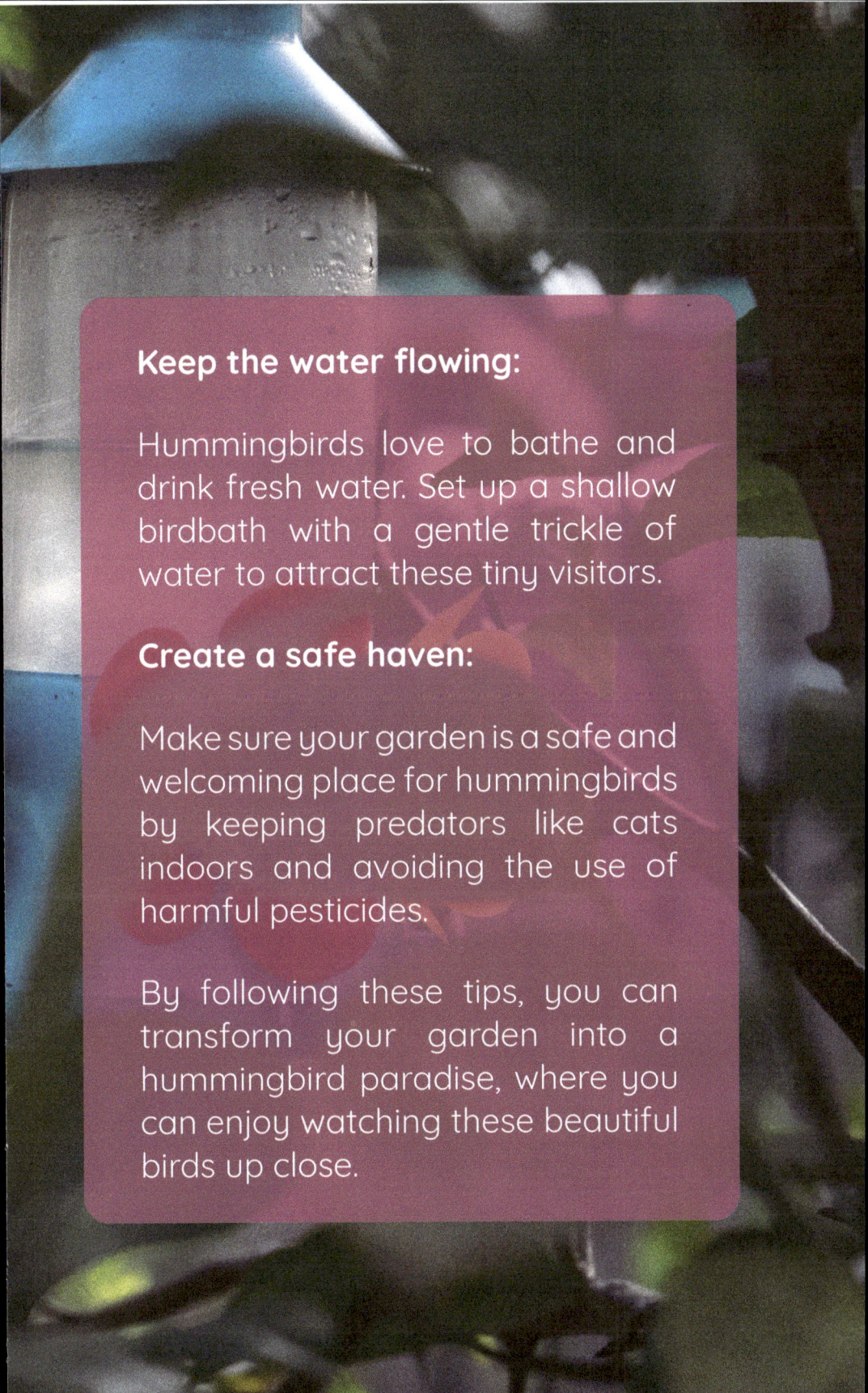

Keep the water flowing:

Hummingbirds love to bathe and drink fresh water. Set up a shallow birdbath with a gentle trickle of water to attract these tiny visitors.

Create a safe haven:

Make sure your garden is a safe and welcoming place for hummingbirds by keeping predators like cats indoors and avoiding the use of harmful pesticides.

By following these tips, you can transform your garden into a hummingbird paradise, where you can enjoy watching these beautiful birds up close.

THE ULTIMATE HUMMINGBIRD BOOK

HUMMINGBIRD FUN FACTS

You've already learned so much about hummingbirds, but there's still more to discover! Prepare to dive into a treasure trove of fascinating and delightful fun facts about hummingbirds.

There are over 340 species of hummingbirds worldwide.

• • •

The smallest hummingbird is the bee hummingbird, which is about 2 inches long and weighs less than 2 grams.

• • •

The largest hummingbird is the giant hummingbird, which can be up to 8.5 inches long and weigh up to 20 grams.

• • •

The average lifespan of a hummingbird is 3 to 5 years, but some have been known to live up to 12 years.

THE ULTIMATE HUMMINGBIRD BOOK

A hummingbird's heart can beat up to 1,260 times per minute.

• • •

Hummingbirds can fly forwards, backwards, and even upside down.

• • •

While most birds have three toes pointing forward and one pointing backward, hummingbirds have two pointing in each direction, which helps them grip branches better.

• • •

Some hummingbird species have a "gorget," which is an iridescent patch of feathers on their throats that appears to change color depending on the angle of light.

The sword-billed hummingbird has a beak longer than its body, which it uses to feed on long-tubed flowers.

• • •

Hummingbirds are known to mate with multiple partners during the breeding season.

• • •

The average clutch size for a hummingbird is just two eggs.

• • •

Hummingbird eggs are tiny, about the size of a pea or small jelly bean.

It takes 14 to 23 days for hummingbird eggs to hatch, depending on the species.

• • •

Baby hummingbirds are born blind and without feathers, but they quickly develop both within a few weeks.

• • •

Some hummingbird species have a "dive display" during courtship, in which they fly high into the air and then swoop down at high speeds to impress a potential mate.

• • •

Hummingbirds have excellent memories and can remember the locations of individual flowers and feeders, as well as when they were last visited.

Hummingbirds can **enter** a state called "torpor" at night, during which their heart rate and body temperature drop significantly to conserve energy.

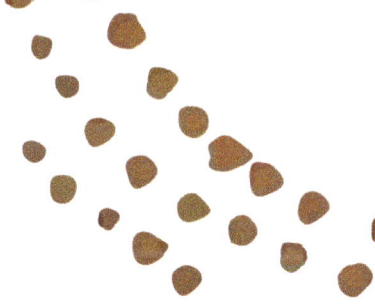

Some species of hummingbirds are known to engage in "nectar robbing," where they pierce the base of a flower to access the nectar without actually pollinating the plant.

• • •

Some hummingbird species can consume up to twice their body weight in nectar every day.

• • •

Hummingbirds have a "crop," which is a small pouch in their throat where they store nectar before it's digested.

The rufous hummingbird has the longest migration route of any hummingbird species, traveling up to 3,000 miles each way between its breeding and wintering grounds.

• • •

Many hummingbird species have specialized relationships with certain flowers, evolving to match the shape and size of their preferred nectar source.

• • •

The hummingbird's hovering ability is due in part to the unique ball-and-socket joint at its shoulder, which allows for a wide range of motion.

Hummingbirds have tiny, lightweight bones that make up only about 10% of their total body weight.

• • •

A hummingbird's tongue is forked and can extend well beyond the tip of its bill, allowing it to reach deep into flowers for nectar.

• • •

Hummingbirds can drink nectar at a rate of 13 licks per second.

• • •

Some hummingbirds have been known to travel as fast as 34 miles per hour in straight, level flight.

A hummingbird's metabolism is among the highest of any bird species, requiring it to consume large amounts of nectar to fuel its energetic lifestyle.

• • •

Hummingbirds are highly territorial and will defend their favorite feeding spots against other hummingbirds and even larger birds.

• • •

The iridescence in hummingbird feathers is created by microscopic platelets in the feathers that refract light, causing the brilliant colors we see.

• • •

Some species of hummingbirds use spider silk to help bind their nests together, making them strong and flexible.

Hummingbirds have very good eyesight and can see ultraviolet light, which is invisible to humans.

• • •

Unlike most birds, hummingbirds cannot walk or hop; they can only perch.

• • •

Hummingbirds are native only to the Americas, ranging from Alaska to Tierra del Fuego.

• • •

The hummingbird's rapid wing beats create a humming sound, which is how they got their name.

Hummingbird beaks are not just used for feeding! They also play a crucial role in their territorial and courtship displays. Males may engage in aerial "beak duels" with other males, using their beaks to assert dominance or to protect their territory.

Many hummingbird species have a "helicopter parent" style of parenting, with the mother doing most of the care for the young, including feeding and keeping them warm.

• • •

Hummingbirds are important pollinators, as they transfer pollen from flower to flower while feeding on nectar.

• • •

Some species of hummingbirds can fly at altitudes of up to 14,000 feet.

• • •

A hummingbird's wings beat around 50 times per second during normal flight, and up to 200 times per second during a courtship display.

The bill of the long-billed hermit hummingbird is curved, allowing it to access the nectar of curved flowers more easily.

• • •

The black-chinned hummingbird has a unique courtship display, in which the male performs a series of pendulum-like swings in front of the female.

• • •

While some species of hummingbirds are highly migratory, others stay in the same general area year-round.

• • •

The violet-crowned woodnymph hummingbird has brilliant green and violet feathers, making it one of the most colorful hummingbird species.

The sapphire-spangled emerald hummingbird gets its name from the bright, jewel-like colors of its feathers, which shine in a dazzling display when the light catches them just right.

Image: Nick Athanas

Hummingbirds have very few natural predators, but they can sometimes fall victim to larger birds, snakes, and even spiders.

• • •

The calliope hummingbird is the smallest bird species in North America, measuring just over 3 inches long.

• • •

Some species of hummingbirds engage in "bill fencing," a behavior in which two birds clash their bills together in a territorial dispute.

• • •

The Andean hillstar hummingbird lives in the high Andes Mountains, where it faces extreme weather conditions and a limited supply of nectar-producing flowers.

THE ULTIMATE HUMMINGBIRD BOOK

Hummingbird QUIZ

Were you paying attention?! Test your new hummingbird knowledge in our quiz!

1. How many species of hummingbirds are there worldwide?

2. What is the smallest hummingbird species called?

3. Which hummingbird species is the largest?

4   How long is the average lifespan of a hummingbird?

5   How fast can a hummingbird's heart beat per minute?

6   In which direction can hummingbirds NOT fly?

7   What is a "gorget"?

8   What is the main source of food for hummingbirds?

9   How long does it take for hummingbird eggs to hatch?

10 What is the name of the state that hummingbirds enter at night to conserve energy?

THE ULTIMATE HUMMINGBIRD BOOK

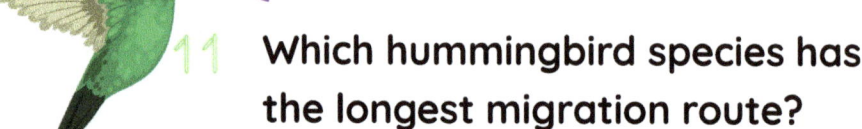

11 **Which hummingbird species has the longest migration route?**

12 **What is special about the joint at a hummingbird's shoulder?**

13 **How do hummingbirds create the iridescence in their feathers?**

14 **What material do some hummingbirds use to help bind their nests together?**

15 **Can hummingbirds see ultraviolet light?**

16 **Where are hummingbirds native to?**

17 **How did hummingbirds get their name?**

18　What role do hummingbirds play in the ecosystem as they feed on nectar?

19　How fast can some hummingbirds travel in straight, level flight?

20　Are hummingbirds territorial?

21　What is unique about the bill of the long-billed hermit hummingbird?

22　Which hummingbird species is the smallest in North America?

ANSWERS

1. Over 340 species
2. Bee hummingbird
3. Giant hummingbird
4. 3 to 5 years
5. Up to 1,260 times per minute
6. They can fly in all directions (forward, backward, and upside down)
7. An iridescent patch of feathers on the throat
8. Nectar
9. 14 to 23 days, depending on the species
10. Torpor
11. Rufous hummingbird
12. The unique ball-and-socket joint
13. By microscopic platelets in the feathers that refract light
14. Spider silk

15. Yes
16. The Americas (from Alaska to Tierra del Fuego)
17. From the humming sound created by their rapid wing beats
18. Pollinators
19. Up to 34 miles per hour
20. Yes
21. It is curved
22. Calliope hummingbird

Can you find all the words below in the word search puzzle on the right?

NECTAR   HOVER   TROCHILIDAE

IRIDESCENT   MIGRATION   GORGET

POLLINATION   TORPOR   HUMMING

HUMMINGBIRDS
WORD SEARCH

A	T	R	O	C	H	I	L	I	D	A	E
D	B	J	G	D	A	B	X	Z	S	D	F
H	I	R	I	D	E	S	C	E	N	T	U
U	G	O	R	G	E	T	J	H	G	O	Y
M	Q	D	D	B	H	C	N	H	F	R	T
M	N	G	D	S	H	O	A	S	S	P	E
I	Q	E	C	H	F	D	V	A	D	O	D
N	Q	S	C	B	T	E	A	E	R	F	R
G	J	G	F	T	S	A	C	B	R	J	G
Q	V	Z	D	G	A	N	Y	E	H	H	H
U	Y	T	M	I	G	R	A	T	I	O	N
A	P	O	L	L	I	N	A	T	I	O	N

THE ULTIMATE HUMMINGBIRD BOOK

SOLUTION

	T	R	O	C	H	I	L	I	D	A	E
H	I	R	I	D	E	S	C	E	N	T	
U	G	O	R	G	E	T				O	
M					H					R	
M	N					O				P	
I		E					V			O	
N			C					E		R	
G			T					R			
				A							
			M	I	G	R	A	T	I	O	N
		P	O	L	L	I	N	A	T	I	O	N

SOURCES

Clark, C. J., & Dudley, R. (2009). Flight costs of long, sexually selected tails in hummingbirds. Proceedings of the Royal Society B: Biological Sciences, 276(1662), 2109-2115. doi:10.1098/rspb.2009.0009

McGuire, J. A., Witt, C. C., Remsen Jr, J. V., Corl, A., Rabosky, D. L., Altshuler, D. L., & Dudley, R. (2014). Molecular phylogenetics and the diversification of hummingbirds. Current Biology, 24(8), 910-916. doi:10.1016/j.cub.2014.03.016

National Audubon Society. (n.d.). Hummingbirds. Retrieved from https://www.audubon.org/birds/hummingbirds

Smithsonian National Museum of Natural History. (n.d.). Hummingbird Facts. Retrieved from https://naturalhistory.si.edu/education/teaching-resources/birds/hummingbird-facts

Stiles, F. G., & Remsen Jr, J. V. (2013). The hummingbird handbook: Everything you need to know about these fascinating birds. Timber Press.

The Cornell Lab of Ornithology. (n.d.). All About Birds. Retrieved from https://www.allaboutbirds.org/guide/browse/hummingbirds

Trochilidae - Hummingbirds. (n.d.). In The Internet Bird Collection. Retrieved from https://www.hbw.com/ibc/family/hummingbirds-trochilidae

United States Fish and Wildlife Service. (n.d.). Hummingbirds. Retrieved from https://www.fws.gov/birds/bird-enthusiasts/backyard/hummingbirds.php

"Hummingbird Summary". 2023. Encyclopedia Britannica. https://www.britannica.com/summary/hummingbird

"Discover 36 Fun Facts About Hummingbirds". 2023. The Spruce. https://www.thespruce.com/fun-facts-about-hummingbirds-387106.

"22 Jaw-Dropping Facts About Hummingbirds". 2022. Birds And Blooms. https://www.birdsandblooms.com/birding/attracting-hummingbirds/13-jaw-dropping-facts-about-hummingbirds/.

"Anna's Hummingbird Courtship Display And Nest Building Observed". 2023. Encyclopedia Britannica. https://www.britannica.com/video/21985/courtship-hummingbird-Anna-display-flight-diving-male.

You're Hum-believable!

As our delightful journey through the world of hummingbirds comes to an end, we hope you've enjoyed learning about these fascinating birds as much as we enjoyed sharing their story with you. Your feedback means a lot to us, so we kindly ask you to **leave a review** on the platform where you purchased the book.

Your thoughts and experiences will help other readers discover the captivating world of hummingbirds and encourage us to continue creating engaging and educational content for all.

Thank you for your support, and may the spirit of these enchanting creatures continue to inspire you!

ALSO BY JENNY KELLETT

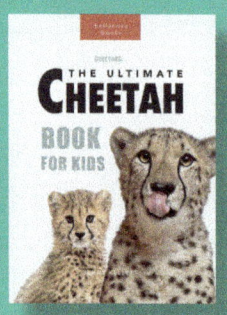

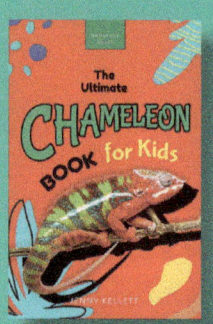

... and more!

Available at
www.bellanovabooks.com
and all major online bookstores.

www.ingramcontent.com/pod-product-compliance
Lightning Source LLC
LaVergne TN
LVHW050842080526
838202LV00009B/318